The Inner Shore

A Poetry Collection from Kelly Buchan

This book is dedicated to Ruby and Buzz,
who are my constant calm in a world of abstract chaos.

*

With gratitude to all of those who've shown me what
love and loss is. You gave me the fuel to begin the
alchemical processes. I wouldn't be who I am now
without our experiences.

*

If not for the words of encouragement from
Mr Shane Levene, this book would never have been
written. Thank you for your poetry Shane.

Contents

Poetry

As Above So Below

Mirrors, mirrors all around,
Mirrors built into the ground.
Mirrors laced into the sky,
Reflecting back the all-seeing eye

Golden ribbons float between,
What we perceive and what's unseen.
Revealing whilst unravelling,
For those who seek the veil lifts clean.

Teeny tiny, twinkling stars,
How'd you get up so very far?
Have you been lonely in the sky?
As you've watched aeons flutter by?

I'd never wish upon a star,
For it matters not what wishes are.
The truth of it is plain to see,
I am the stars and they are me.

2022

He Hums a Sad Song

I cut myself
On the broken pieces of you,
We tried to mend.
And poured the blood,
Into countless letters
I hadn't the courage to send.
There's no respite
From the silent void,
Or echoes of you to be found.
I left you on the rotting floor,
As you drowned
in your own sad sound.

2022

Breaking Her Curse

I guess it's hard not to be hopeful,
As we're floating in my bed.
Your shadow cloaks us gently,
And my magick stains us red.

She consumed you long ago,
But you're loving me instead.
I hope that soon she'll fade from view,
As we slow dance 'round your head.

I guess it's hard not to be hopeful,
As we roll around this bed,
We fuck inside-out and back again,
Like dogs that haven't been fed.

What horrors were spouted that hurt you so?
Or is it the words you left unsaid?
You're looking straight through me
And into her soul,
As we sacrifice my bed.

Am I the one you've always dreamed of?
Are mine the only legs you'll spread?
Or is she out there on your periphery?
Holding her curse that chains you dead.

I guess it's hard not to be hopeful,
That your heart hasn't fully been bled.
I guess it's hard not to be grateful,
That you're loving me instead.

2021

Poimandres

Is it you, oh mind, who sees it all?
Are you the breath behind the matter?
Was it you, oh mind, who birthed the fire?
Was it as enchanting as you remember?
Through the shadows, oh mind, the eye became,
And gave birth to the eyes who make fractals.
Share your glorious secrets,
Oh creator, oh mind.
From where did you pull forth the ether?
Is it you, oh mind, that whispers it still?
In the land where thoughts become matter?
If you are Poimandres, please grant me the key,
My illusions are pleading to shatter.

2022

Don't Ask The Moon

I wrote a song the other day,
And gave it to the moon.
In hopes she'd read it over,
And whisper me the tune.

"Oh darling girl", she said to me,
"Your words are out of sorts,
I can't gift you a melody,
When your heart is bound in knots".

"I can give you moonlight,
And cosmic dreams galore.
But your heart's desire can't come from me,
Don't ask me anymore."

I took my song just yesterday,
And gave it to the sun.
With a yawning smile he closed his eyes,
And sang a slow wee hum.

"My darling girl," he said to me,
"This isn't any use,
Your heart has lost It's beat you see,
It's had too much abuse."

"Music doesn't come from searching

Outside in the dark.
Look within to find it…
You should maybe ask your heart."

So I took my song this morning,
And I tried to find my heart.
T'was engulfed in flames and clotted blood,
Like a dreadful piece of art.

"My darling girl," she sobbed at me.
"Please tell me that we're done.
How many times must you squeeze me dry?
This isn't any fun."

I cleaned her up as best I could,
And showered her with praise.
Her beat restarted readily,
But her wistful eyes were glazed.

"Remember when we danced til dawn,
And sang of hope and grace?
Why must it always come to an end?
I hate this awful place."

I lulled her into a slumber,
To let her rest once more.
And I asked the moon and sun
To help her heal her open sores.

Then I took my selfish little song,
And burned it 'neath the moon.
My broken heart can't catch its breath,
To whisper me the tune.

2021

Sleep Tight, Little Star

*Written in memory of the beautiful Margo Jean Wheeler, who
was born sleeping on the 23rd October 2022.*

The angels sang too early,
When they shone their holy light,
On a face so pure and perfect,
That it blazoned up the night.

No words could ever prepare us,
To lose a soul so small and bright.
You're a star that will glow on forever,
As you sparkle with all of your might.

It it true that you cannot come with us,
And our path now seems unclear,
But we'll find you in every rainbow,
And we'll feel you whenever you're near.

Margo, you'll live on within us,
As a beacon of all we hold dear.
We'll dream of you under the starlight,
Loving you more with each passing year.

2022

Vagrant Heart

It's bold of you,
To assume that I care,
About your rampant, vagrant heart.
Red flags were fluttering warily,
From before the very start.
You cast my love asunder,
In the most narcissistic way,
Your nihilism was brooding on words,
You didn't care to say.

You had laid to rest our carcass,
Before I realised we'd died.
I was too busy stoking
The fire we had lit,
To notice you roaming outside.
Now all that's left are the ashes,
Of a love that tore me apart.
And all that there is left of you,
Is a rampant, vagrant heart.

2022

Day Five

I cried myself to sleep until,
I cried myself awake.
Recoiling within cracking bones,
My sanity's at stake.

Around and round and round they run,
Hot needles playing games,
The pain howls up in torrents,
Using nerves as climbing frames.

Pointless words cannot describe,
The searing, ugly heat.
For hours I burst with careful tears,
At my body's harsh defeat.

And if you don't know back pain,
You're the lucky one for sure.
Just one more ounce of torment,
And I'll scream forevermore.

2022

The Interlude

I've been a little bit depressed lately.
And that's not an easy thing to admit to a sea of
beautiful souls.
There's been nowhere to hide with the sun shining so.
I've been flinching against the summer frivolities.
My very core is yearning for solitude.

I've been secretly drowning within poised panic
attacks.
It's an odd thing, to be violently losing grip on reality,
To the melody of giggles from the garden.
Only the bumblebees and butterflies at the window,
Have been privy to the silent screams.

As I'm propelled ever onwards,
Inching quicker and closer to the autumnal years of
life,
I'm tortured with visions of cripping lonliness,
And ideas of being lost within an unforgiving winter.
Witness only to my own self loathing,
My reaching arms, finding no one in the dark.

Where once frothed an ocean of tumultuous desire,
My inner shores now lay silent and haunted,
By the ghosts of lovers who've swum my depths.
My waters are stifled, gasping for air.
Aching for a singular stone to be cast,
Waiting for the slightest gift of a nudge,
That will herald an end,
To this perpetual interlude.

2021

Moon Gazing

I'll try not to pick apart your heart,
While gazing at your moon.
It's a whispering soliloquy,
Your brilliant white monsoon.
You bathe us in the purest light,
Your moonshine soft and lilting,
Silvery strands of secret songs,
Leave my silent shadows wilting.
Encased within your moonbeams,
I fold straight into the sky.
So I'll try not to pick apart your heart,
As I fall into your eyes.

2022

The Pity Party

Do the consequences of your actions haunt you quite a
bit?
Since you were thinking you could act however you
see fit.
Did the lies you told get tangled up to form a choking
noose?
Your rotten soul it reeks of all the second hand abuse.

Oh what a shame! Your bad deeds hit you right back
in your face!
Does it hurt you that the whole world knows and
sings of your disgrace?
A mess of bloody war torn hearts is strewn across your
floor,
For you to stare at endlessly, while the wolves pound
at your door.

This false contrition suits you sir, you wear it like a
mask.
You're so spiritually bankrupt, even smiling is a task.
The pity party's over dear, it's all come to a head.
Go find a lesser mortal soul, and cry to her instead.

2022

Sex Magick

Waves begin to break in rhythmic swells,
With backs arched in tightening awe.
Searching fingertips find heavy hidden groans,
As ankles grip and beckon the crescendo.

Intertwined still, they bend and they sway,
Each using the other as a cosmic ladder.
Climbing up and closer to the yawning pleasure,
A purple wormhole heralds the abyss.

Falling through kaleidoscopic convulsions,
An eternity is cloaked in a jolting embrace.
There's a quiet comprehension of the darkness,
It serves to let the magick birth the light.

Lovers folded up in secret creases.
As breathless prayers evaporate from skin.
There's starlight shining through each glistening pore,
Our twisted bodies lay in the dawning afterglow.

2022

The Artist

A lackadaisical thrum fills the smoke stained air,
As calluses chime against fretboards.
Music notes twinkle and fall like the stars,
They're mapping a way home to you.
It's like our lives are binary,
Two souls held apart.
But a fated trajectory guides me straight home,
To your magnetic heart.

2022

The Precipice

I'd rather keep you in my mind…
For now…I think…
It's easier to not fall in,
If your love is just a figment
Of my twisted imagination.

I'll lock you out my forlorn heart…
For now…I think…
I'll keep you a fading memory,
One that sighs
As it wisps out of sight.

I'll have to forget you even exist…
For now…I think…
Except maybe when I hear a melody,
That carries your ghost right on in.

I'm taking this no further…
For now…I think…
That's an awfully big chasm to jump,
And I'm not nearly as brave as I once was.

I'll take a piece of you with me…
My love…please know…
A lucky totem of yours to keep,
While our hearts leave this behind.

I'll visit you in my dreams…
My love…I know for sure…
We'll stand at the precipice together,
Both knowing neither one of us will jump.

2022

Calcifer

Palid blues where reds once roared,
A spark blinks out of sight.
There's no notes for licking flames to dance,
Like lovers through the night.

Flickers fight the subtle hiss,
Of a dying heart's last song.
She listens close to it's quaking light,
"I'll see you soon…It won't be long…"

As Calcifer looks through her eyes,
The last of him starts burning.
With a grieving sigh she whispers back,
"A heart's a heavy burden".

2022

Nine of Swords

Have you ever felt sadness full of hate and abrasion?
It's an ominous place, an eternal damnation.
It burns in me now as I pray for salvation.
Desolation must be the harshest vibration.

My painted on face is a sad hallucination,
Pretty colours and trinkets can't feign real elation.
Loneliness looms and completes the equation,
And I'm locked once again into glum isolation.

The girl in my head, she wails in frustration,
She bangs on my walls in stark desperation.
Why can't I halt her atrocious narration?
She tells me that solitude is my fated destination.

But a glimmer of sunlight hails my latest fixation,
Could it be? An end to this intrinsic stagnation?
Weeks skip on past with flirtatious titillation,
Love filters in and we bask in exaltation.

I tried to let go of all past violations.
It's just so hard to swim in mental aggravation,
So of course he pulls back, resuming the starvation,
Leaving me drowning in weak protestations.

Have you ever felt sadness full of hate and abrasion?
It's an ominous place, an eternal damnation.
It burns in me now as I pray for salvation.
Desolation must be the harshest vibration.

2021

The Inner Shore

Come meet me below,
Where the loneliness grows,
In tendrils that choke over time.
It's quiet down there,
Only memories crash,
In rhythms without any rhyme.

Down there, there's a shore,
Where a bitter taste swells,
Waves froth in an unspent swoon.
The silence, it seethes,
As the solitude, breathes,
By the light of my marauding moon.

2022

The Poison Tree

Let's embark on our loathsome pilgrimage,
To repent at the base of the poison tree.
I'll bear witness to the grim, gruesome ritual,
As it drinks you dry darkly, and spits you out cold.

Your tongue is brazen and barbed my love,
Sitting proud within liquor laced lips.
Was it born from the fruit of the poison tree?
It sure creeps with the same kind of rot.

Intertwined we could weep black and deeply,
Under branches with leaves limp with death.
Into abstract rejection, we'll writhe and dissolve,
With neither one of us saving the other.

Becoming one with the roots of the poison tree,
Searching fingertips, gnarled out of reach.
Our souls twisted and tortured, frozen in time,
As it drinks us down darkly, and swallows us whole.

2021

Puff Of Smoke

A heart lays on a butchers block,
And it's coughing out splinters of lead.
It wimpers alone, like a dying old dog,
Who's waiting for a blow to the head.

A sickness is seeping, quiet and calm,
No music notes hang in the air.
The butcher advances, baring his teeth,
To rip apart all that was shared.

It didn't take a magick wand,
Or a whispered spell bespoke.
All at once in a single, strangled cry,
You were gone in a puff of smoke.

2022

The Silicone Veil

It's a tenuous grip
That we all seem to have,
On this most subjective of stages.
No-one seems to know,
How to reap and then sow.
To exploit as we fall through the pages.

This life is a game,
We all play step by step
With each chapter bound tightly in time.
We all have to learn,
To play nice and in turn,
And accept that we're truly divine.

2022

The Void

I watched it happen.
Your heavy vaulted door,
Slamming in slow motion.
I wanted to scramble frantically.
To try to salvage empty sobs.
But I couldn't save a fated love,
That was never even mine.
So instead I watched on,
As you voiced no protestations.
Your heart's chamber closing,
Without so much as an echo.
Locked out of your love,
And screaming into a darkness,
That won't even whisper back.

2022

We Hate It When We Feel Like This

A poem dedicated to Scott Hutchison

On the days that I've woken up hurting,
With life's glare burning sore in my eyes,
My crippled heart lurches towards them,
To the words he wove into our skies.

There's been whispers of tiny wee changes,
Of human heat birthing slivers of light.
Lyrics ooze an oil slick of memories,
He's with us all as we swim through the night.

Scottish hearts howled and dissolved then,
When the lonely man made his last sound.
The misery of love was resounding.
Not a trace of the leper was found.

He's been my navigation through as the north sea
swells.
His words crafting tunnels in the myre.
His voice beacons out across the black and the cold,
His heart, the only spark to light the pyre.

We can pray that he's resting up easy.
And we can hope that his corner is bright.
But alas, all I can be is grateful,
To the man whose soul helped mine take flight.

Hopeful Souls

Something about him sticks in my mind,
Like a memory I've yet to experience.
Melodies condense from the sound of his voice,
And sing songs that have longed to be written.

So much to learn from those wise eyes of his,
Blues and browns running ancient and deep.
He placed a seed in my hand, and whispered so low,
"What grows is under your keep."

I take flight with the stars, while he's rooted down
firm,
Holding space for our tentative spark.
A connection divine, linking his light to mine.
May this love lead us out of the dark.

2022

Five of Cups

An anti-climactic crescendo roars,
As puzzle pieces melt,
Like grey ash in muddy rain.
I'm pining deep within the loneliness,
Perhaps I'll wallow here
For just a moment longer,
Dreaming of soft kisses
That never truly formed.
My heart gives out a twitch,
And spins like a marble
Within my empty chest.
Just how cruel must my tortured mind be,
For it to keep conjuring sudden memories,
Of how your skin smells
In the dark?

2022

Amun-Ra

A most wrathful god like no other,
He glares piercingly from the sky.
We offer up at the solstices,
To gain favour in his eye.

He's made of looping knots of fire,
And protruding tongues of heat.
We're gifted overflowing cosmic soup,
From the god who never sleeps.

Broiling hellscapes twist and morph,
While weeping valves release,
He's the most wise omniscient being,
Who can bring mankind to its knees.

Witches dance beneath his splendor,
Offering souls like slabs of meat.
Merry go rounds of feminine wiles,
Find a way to sing discreet.

A screaming deity spanning aeons,
May his mercy never fade.
For Amun-Ra burns ever more,
As we flail beneath his gaze.

2021

An Elixir For The Broken Hearted

Brave and bitter hearts transmute
The most powerful poetry.
Alchemising sonnets serve
To seep a subtle comfort,
Like words spinning hunger into
Grains of spiritual sustenance.
They feed something that's unverbalised,
Yet felt in its entirety.

When sentences are forged from
The very lowest of vibrations,
They sing true of that feeling when
You're standing all alone.
Peering straight down the road,
Leading into a nightmare,
And watching the streetlights
Blink out one by one.

2022

Midnight Mushrooms

I slide backwards through the reality shift.
Falling into the world you cannot unsee.
An alchemical brew begins boiling internally.
God is being spun into beads of gold.

Bowing down before the almighty, all-seeing eye.
I watch myself soar within its swirling iris.
Can it give me the answers I so desperately seek?
As I wander, it blinks back.

It sits on a web of the most sacred geometry,
With mechanisms twisting and furling eternally.
I ride the psychedelic waves that never seem to break.
And then melt into myself like wax.

Eyes give birth to triangles within squares.
Inviting me into its fractal vortex.
A consciousness moves behind the forms.
it sings through the veil in etheric tones.

Unifying secrets are whispered beneath,
Spoken in a language of pulsating patterns.
The ego's reborn, stripped away from the lense.
I am the eye, and It's looking at me.

2022

Four Out Of Six

And so it was.
Another one gone.
No reassuring heartbeat.
Devoid of flickering life.
Just an empty dark screen,
Mirroring my broken heart.

And so it began,
Roaring rivers ran red.
I said farewell to the
Fading sunrises which
Never broke dawn.
They were sparks of hope
That were lost to the stars,
And swallowed whole by blood.

And so it is now,
No faces to obsess over,
Or dog-earred photographs to cherish.
Just an echoing thump,
A fatal totality,
And the breathless gasp
Of a half-forgotten nightmare.

Here I am today,
Wading through daydreams.
Barely a mother,
But so very grateful.
For the precious lives,
Of my daughter and son,
Who effortlessly feed my soul honey,
When I'm too sad to even cry.

2021

Daddy Dearest

For my dear friend Laura Morrice, in memory of her beloved father, Sandy Milne.

The time has come for you to go,
Oh dad, I wish it wasn't so.
Your light has shone so bright for years,
It's shining now, but through my tears.

Your blood, it courses in my veins,
And warms me through like summer rain.
Your wisdom dad, will stay with me.
And guide me for eternity.

As the children grow, I'll think of you,
And the ways in which you followed through,
On the sacred contracts parents sign,
To pass on love so pure, divine.

Daddy dearest, rest your heart,
And know we'll never be apart.
For your love shines just like the stars,
And fills my soul with who you are.

2022

Crunch

All at once,
There came a noise.
Ungodly and encompassing.
In less than the blink of an eye,
It hit me where I couldn't go.
A crunch so loud and sickening,
It knocked me out clean.

And now,
Alone, I lay at night.
The noise repeating
Through my skull.
And I just can't help but wonder,
From where the sound really came.
Was it a symptom of the chaos outside?
Or a holler from my startled bones?

2022

Daisy Chains

I know this isn't normal,
Or a healthy thing to do.
I can't quite help but spend my midnights
Daydreaming of you.

I made you daisy chains of love notes,
They were hand inscribed with wishes.
I placed them all into a box,
And sealed it up with kisses.

But now i hate the way my stomach drops,
When the wind whispers your name.
Won't someone tell the universe,
That I quit it's cosmic game?

These daisy chains of sadness,
Are choking down my heart.
They're inducing waking nightmares,
Where my love is ripped apart.

I know this isn't healthy,
But there's not much left to do.
Our memories loom like spectres,
Haunting me with thoughts of you.

2022

Haiku Poetry

I prayed to the gods

To be happy once again.

They got rid of him.

Squares of wise Poets

A digital honeycomb

Of those who impart.

Written for Fin Hall, host of poetry event Like a Blot from the Blue

Who could deny him?

His sharp eyes drip with moonlight.

They soak me right through.

Urgent bodies writhe,

Fingers mark her pale ripe thighs.

He bites her soft lip.

The sweet sacrifice,

Of virgins brought to slaughter,

As the moon howls full.

I've no real reason,

To doubt the lessons I've learnt.

It's a shame they've hurt.

Six cups sit thirsty.

Their emptiness calling true,

For a soul long loved.

To let our moons drip,

Against the humdrum of life,

Was a privilege.

I'll burn some letters,

And pray 'neath the next full moon.

Turning us to dust.

You can break my heart,

But not my disposition.

Not today, darling

That look in his eye,

Leaves my heart pounding harder.

Than an uncut drug.

Shimmering embers.

From the bluest eyes i've seen.

Let's see if they'll glow.

I belong up there.

Swimming with the golden stars.

Lost in the abyss.

A tender sweet kiss,

Within your brooding shadow,

Would soothe these wounds so.

Short Stories and Prose

The Goddess and The Poetaster

The subtle sweetness of your voice is my current drug of choice, and it ebbs and flows against all of my better judgements. Sitting poised with the phone, I grow agitated with the sound of my own breath. It's drowning you out and I don't want to miss a single second we spend in our own personal timeline.

There's something so remarkably soothing about the spaces between your words. Small pauses of content reflection waft through the silent smiles that I can sense beneath the undertows of conversation. With eyes closed I plunge into your warmth, although it radiates from much too many miles away.

You really are a waking overdose my darling. A lover in the night too fragile to touch, yet much too alluring to run from. I'm prepping myself for a loss. Almost crystallizing small bursts of feeling so that I mourn your attention when it inevitably wanes and floats off, along with my dissipating sanity.

I've been driven to a point beyond the horizon, staring back at a starting block I no longer recognise, while the night ahead looms dark and lonely. Living in a fantasy will only ever serve one purpose, and the fear of being dropped and discarded into the black is a feeling that's too overwhelming to stomach.

Yet still, my love. There you are in all of your tragic glory. Emanating a promise that all could be well with the world should one only believe in divine and fated love. What a horrible shame it is then, that our lives could never entangle themselves in the same way as I'm tangled up in the idea of being your 'one'.

Street Corner Blues

First featured in Fin Hall's Joined Up Writing: Three Fall

On a particularly dreich winter's night, a small man stood staring on a street corner. The blue winds bit and chewed at his flesh as he searched in vain for his long gone marbles. Unfortunately for him, they had fled with the better weather.

Fraserburgh has a lot to answer for. Husks of humans roam the grotty streets, their insides as hollow as the town itself. The only town plaza is a designated meeting point. There stands a rusting statue of a long forgotten figure. The statue's gaze takes in all the abhorrent goings on, with nicotine yellow street lights regretfully illuminating the despair.

The small man was oblivious to the gaggle of heroin addicts who were robbing the corner shop adjacent to him. Not a grimace graced his gnarled face as the howls of an enraged shopkeeper came muffled through the door. He just stood. Feet glued to the pavement by years of unfathomable depression and loneliness. It was a heaviness too thick to consider. He just stood.

Chaos began spewing from the corner shop. Confusion and anger echoed round the square as the small man just stood staring. He gave no reaction as they roared past him with pockets full of sweets, fags, and the pathetic contents of the shopkeepers till. His face remained expressionless as he was knocked to the ground by the last of the assailants. Nor did it alter when his skull met the pavement with the same tone as a rotten coconut.

The only thing that changed for the small man as he lay staring on the street corner, was the resonant question pounding through his cracked and leaking head.

"What kind of fated destiny is this?"

The Fallacy of Online Relationships.

Thirty-six hours was all it took for the madness to set in proper. I felt myself being inextricably pulled through time and space to lay with a stranger whom I couldn't even be sure existed.

All it took was a superficial message of kindness and a common ground of ideologies, miseries and experiences. Twenty-seven messages was all I needed to dive headfirst into a digital infatuation.

My physical body carried on with the mundane dance of daily duties as my soul flew through the ether to find him. We lay forehead to forehead within the astral, staring into our reflective abysses for hours upon end. Our manufactured reality belonged only to us as we signed ourselves over to each other for not much in return.

I felt his essence wrap around mine, and was being possessed by a ghost of my own making. We spent lifetimes together within my mind's eye. Rollercoasting between love and lunacy and lust and obsession. The connection felt so real and so visceral, that falling in heart first was inevitable. He permeated my thoughts to such an extent, he became a disembodied narrator, guiding me through my day whilst gently stroking my ego.

My primal instincts told me to hold on tight, although I knew deep down we could never really be.
My heart told me that he was the one, an idea which will forever cause a dull thump to ring through my bones.
My head told me to get a fucking therapist.

You Should Go On Tinder

"Have you ever been on Tinder?"

Hannah smirked at me between indulgent puffs of her afternoon cigarillo.

"You should try it doll, you need to get laid."

I wrinkled my nose at the thought of slapping myself with a *For Sale* sign and joining the never ending gallery of lonely souls and broken hearts. A sad square on a shit app, that's what I'd be. Shining out in search of any form of attention, painted over with a happy face. What could I even write as a description of myself? Must I condense my entire being into 40 poetic characters in order to hook and line my one true love? These bio lines have always reeked of a certain despondent desperation anyhow.

Murderously fucked over goddess incarnate seeking nothing less than the epitome of the masculine divine.

"How's that?" I grinned. Hannah grabbed my phone, and within 45 seconds she had me virtually up for grabs. I was thus presented with a catalog of local bachelors, each one's profile formatted to be stacked on top of the others like a deck of cards. Classifieds on my screen that I proceeded to bin off at my leisure.

Gary, 43, 7km away.
"What's the difference between me and my sofa? My sofa pulls out."

Mindaugas, 40, 2km away.
"Don't bother matching if you have fake tits or lip filler."

Will, 29, 11km away.
"I like my lovers like I like my coffee. So if you're hot and bitter, swipe right."

Ben, 32, 5km away.
"Always up for a laugh, Man Utd daft."

Shaun, 36, 15km away.
"Looking for no strings attached fun...a 9 inch cock...can keep secrets..."

Jonny, 42, 7km away.
"I'm a dick, that's just how I roll."

Robert, 34, 40km away.
"I work in oil and gas and drive an Audi A3."

Roy, 42, 61km away.

"I like my women like I like my spider webs, symmetrical with a little bit of sag."

Their countless eyes made me feel suddenly sick. Men I wouldn't spit on for a fiver were now able to give me a rating out of ten. Mirroring the gaggle of receding hairlines, a pack of painfully forced biceps and heavily chiseled abdominal muscles were dancing a strange peacock dance. I don't really care for such physiques, there's nothing warm and comforting about them. It's like trying to cuddle a bed frame. And anyway, with 6 pregnancies and two children under my belt, a real life meeting would be sure to end in disappointment for them. An airbrushed instagram beauty eager to inflate egos and erections raised on anal porn, I am not.

"I won't find a soulmate on here."

"You don't need a soulmate honey." Hannah replied in the most sage like way. "You just need your hole filled."

I considered her answer for a moment longer than necessary as I fingered through the virtual pile of offerings. Each face I imagined looking back into mine in the throes of a passionate embrace. I thought of body heat and searching tongues. Of sticky fingertips finding stickier holes. I thought of expressions contorted mid petit mort. And of grunts and moans and whispers through the night. My mind eventually settled on the afterglow. The blissful silence that beams so loudly over entangled lovers who have just signed their hopeful souls over to one another so freely.

My chest thudded emptily as I realised just how much I missed the smell and touch of a masculine body. For something that was meant to be a fun distraction, spending five minutes on Tinder made me feel so much worse. Loneliness filled the hollow space beneath my ribs. I just sat with it quietly, allowing it to undulate as flashes of past lovers made me dizzy with an odd sexual nostalgia.

With all of this in mind, I swiftly deactivated my Tinder account, and threw my phone to the other side of the sofa. I think I'll look for a divine soulmate elsewhere.

The End of the Line

If the faded track marks on his body were a map, they would lead to a place more terrible and depraved than any non drug user could even imagine. The veins underneath his roving scars were no longer visible, having collapsed under the weight of tens of thousands of punctures. His forearms had served as his first masochistic battleground, and now the wilted muscles residing there would flex and distort as he scribbled tales of misery and half truths onto smoke stained paper.

Love letters that never held any meaning at all sailed from one hopeful heart to another. Each of them painting an exquisite mask designed to lure the other one in. His loyalty to gear and the subsequent debauchery however, would always prove to be stronger than potential love. Especially when the threat to his daily routines and habits became suddenly real. A long stark road up to Scotland ends in a churning abyss of not knowing if he could find a stable enough drug supply to rely upon for however long he found himself there.

By the light on his moon, she would swoon to the sound of his engorged poetry. All the while his mind remained in self-induced squalor, running through every scenario that could possibly go wrong with their fledgling love affair. His junked up heart was begging him not to put it up for sale once more, for fear the pain of another round of sorrow and disappointment would ultimately prove too much for him to bear.

An innocence shone from her eyes which illuminated his pock-marked heroin laced existence. Knowing he couldn't keep his house of cards from falling, he braced himself to say a sentence that he knew would shatter this illusion for good.

"I'm still using," he whispered, almost hoping she wouldn't hear.

A pause settled into their atmosphere. Brooding clouds began to billow within her, and her reply made him ache with all the dejection of a thousand broken hearts.

"But darling," she cried softly. "What then if you die and take all of my colours with you?"

Printed in Great Britain
by Amazon

12315948R00041